THE ULTIMATE
TOTTENHAM HOTSPUR
FC TRIVIA BOOK

A Collection of Amazing Trivia Quizzes and Fun
Facts for Die-Hard Spurs Fans!

Ray Walker

Exclusive Free Book

Crazy Sports Stories

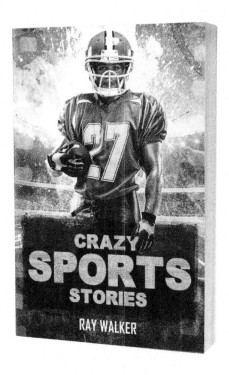

As a thank you for getting a copy of this book I would like to offer you a free copy of my book Crazy Sports Stories which comes packed with interesting stories from your favorite sports such as Football, Hockey, Baseball, Basketball and more.

Grab your free copy over at
RayWalkerMedia.com/Bonus

CONTENTS

INTRODUCTION

It's amazing that a group of schoolboys and cricket players could form what would become one of Britain's premier soccer clubs, way back in 1882, and have it still going strong almost 150 years later. The Tottenham Hotspur story is a fascinating one, and we're about to tell it to you in a lighthearted manner via trivia and facts.

Since becoming the first and only non-league team to hoist the famous FA Cup to the 2020-21 season, Tottenham Hotspur has consistently been making headlines across the UK and Europe.

The club, which started as Hotspur FC, has evolved from playing on public marshes, to the famous White Hart Lane, and now to one of England's newest state-of-the-art stadiums.

The team has topped its league several times and won numerous pieces of silverware over the years due to tremendous passion, commitment, and effort. They're certainly not finished, though, because Premier League titles and European Champions League trophies are still set firmly in their sights.

Nicknamed the "Lilywhites," the club has never played below the second tier of English football, due to its never-ending work ethic, both on and off the pitch. The side is second to none when it comes to entertaining its fans, week in and week out, and it's greatly appreciated.

The Spurs were the first British team to strike gold in a major European tournament back in the 1960s by capturing the European Cup Winners' Cup, and they then became the first domestic side to hoist two European titles.

The team's supporters have witnessed some of the world's top players and managers on the pitch since 1882, with some of the most memorable being: Clive Allen, Bobby Buckle, Ray Clemence, Garth Crooks, Jimmy Dimmock, Paul Gascoigne, Jimmy Greaves, Glenn Hoddle, Gary Lineker, Alan Mullery, Bill Nicholson, Steve Perryman, Martin Peters, Bobby Smith, Dave Mackay, Pat Jennings, David Ginola, Ossie Ardiles, and Harry Kane.

This trivia and fact book has been written to celebrate the absorbing history of Tottenham Hotspur FC, and to re-live all of the unforgettable moments. You'll be able to read about the club's greatest members and how every one of them made an impact with this fascinating outfit.

The Tottenham journey is presented in an entertaining and fun manner with 12 unique chapters each representing a different topic. Each chapter includes 20 spellbinding quiz questions and 10 engrossing "Did You Know" facts. The questions are presented in 15 multiple-choice and 5 true-or-false options with the answers given on a separate page.

Reading this Tottenham Hotspur quiz book is an ideal way to challenge yourself and others on the enthralling history of the club. You'll be well prepared to take on all the Spurs' quiz challenges as well as spread the word about your favorite soccer team at the same time.

CHAPTER 1:

ORIGINS & HISTORY

QUIZ TIME!

1. What year was Tottenham Hotspur FC founded?

   a. 1892

   b. 1888

   c. 1882

   d. 1878

2. The club was originally named Hotspur FC.

   a. True

   b. False

3. What was the first league Tottenham played in professionally?

   a. The Combination

   b. The Football League

   c. The Football Alliance

   d. The Southern League

4. The club's first recorded match was a 2-0 loss to which team?

   a. West Ham United
   b. Leyton Athletics
   c. Arsenal FC
   d. The Radicals

5. Which year did the outfit move to White Hart Lane Stadium?

   a. 1903
   b. 1899
   c. 1895
   d. 1890

6. What was the original shirt color Tottenham played in?

   a. Sky blue
   b. White
   c. Navy blue
   d. Red

7. Tottenham has been relegated four times as of 2020.

   a. True
   b. False

8. the Spurs became the first British team to wear what?

   a. Long-cut shorts
   b. Winter gloves
   c. Long-sleeve shirts
   d. A different colored shirt for the goalkeeper

9. What team did the Spurs play in their first competitive match in the London Association Cup in 1885?

    a. Royal Arsenal

    b. St. Albans

    c. West Ham United

    d. Leyton Orient FC

10. How many games did the team win in its first season in the Football League?

    a. 14

    b. 17

    c. 20

    d. 26

11. Tottenham's first Premier League match was against which side?

    a. Southampton FC

    b. Manchester United

    c. Crystal Palace FC

    d. Leeds United

12. The bird featured on Tottenham's crest is a pheasant.

    a. True

    b. False

13. How many games did the Spurs win in their first Premier League season?

    a. 13

    b. 22

c. 10

d. 16

14. What does the club motto translate to in English?

   a. Those who dare are victorious

   b. Walk with pride

   c. To dare is to do

   d. Risk favors the bold

15. Against which squad did Tottenham win its first Premier League game?

   a. Queens Park Rangers

   b. Liverpool FC

   c. Sheffield United

   d. Everton FC

16. Tottenham's original crest design was an "H" in a red shield.

   a. True

   b. False

17. How many games did the side win in its first season in the Southern League?

   a. 5

   b. 9

   c. 12

   d. 16

18. What was the first season the club was relegated?

   a. 1910-11

   b. 1914-15

c. 1927-28

d. 1934-35

19. The team beat which club 4-1 in its first friendly match at White Hart Lane?

   a. Blackburn Rovers

   b. Manchester City FC

   c. Queens Park Rangers

   d. Notts County

20. The name Hotspur was adopted because of the town's history of forging tools such as horseshoes and the Spurs.

   a. True

   b. False

QUIZ ANSWERS

1. C – 1882

2. A – True

3. D – The Southern League

4. D – The Radicals

5. B – 1899

6. C – Navy Blue

7. A – True

8. A – Long-cut shorts

9. B – St. Albans

10. C – 20

11. A – Southampton FC

12. B – False

13. D – 16

14. C – To dare is to do

15. C – Sheffield United

16. A – True

17. B – 9

18. B – 1914-15

19. D – Notts County

20. B – False

DID YOU KNOW?

1. The Tottenham Hotspur Football Club is located in London, England, and plays in the country's top-tier Premier League. The team's nickname is the Lilywhites, but most fans simply refer to the squad as the Spurs. The majority owner has been ENIC International Ltd. since 2001, and the current chairman is Daniel Levy.

2. The club was originally founded on Sept. 5, 1882, as the Hotspur FC, officially renaming themselves as the Tottenham Hotspur Football Club in 1884. The Hotspur FC was formed by young members of the Hotspur Cricket Club and a local grammar school, with Bobby Buckle as one of the organizers. In 1883, a bible class teacher from All Hallows Church, named John Ripsher, was the club's president and the team's colors were navy blue. The squad played its home games on the public Tottenham Marshes land at the time.

3. Sir Henry Percy was an English knight who was nicknamed "Hotspur" as a tribute to his readiness for attack. Percy allegedly dug the spurs into his horse to make it go faster during his many battles. In addition, the Spurs are associated with fighting cocks. The club featured the Spurs as a symbol in 1900 and the symbol evolved into a fighting cock. It's believed the club was named after Percy

as his descendants owned land close to the Tottenham Marshes.

4. The first recorded match of the Hotspur FC was in September 1882 against a team named the Radicals, which resulted in a 2-0 defeat. The first known competitive match came against St. Albans in the London Association Cup in October 1885, with the Spurs winning 5-2. In addition, the team colors were changed to light blue and white halves.

5. In 1888, the team began playing its home matches at a private venue in Northumberland Park where fans were asked to pay a small admission fee. Two years later, the team colors were changed once again, this time to red shirts with navy blue shorts. In 1892 the side played briefly in the Southern Alliance League.

6. The club turned professional in December 1895, and a year later it was elected to the Southern League Division One where the kit colors were changed to brown and gold. The Spurs reached their first cup final in 1897 when they were beaten 2-0 by Wellingborough in the local Charity Cup event.

7. Tottenham Hotspur became a limited company in 1898 and the side's kit changed again, this time to white shirts with blue shorts. In 1899, the Spurs moved to a venue that eventually held nearly 80,000 fans and was originally planned to be named Gilpin Park. However, the disused nursery owned by the brewers Charrington soon became

known as High Road ground or White Hart grounds and then White Hart Lane. The team's first official match there was a 4-1 friendly win over Notts County.

8. In 1899-1900, the club won the Southern League title and a year later it captured the FA Cup in a replay, becoming the first and only non-league side to win it since the English Football League was formed in 1888. The team didn't enter the Second Division of the Football League until 1908, however. It earned promotion to the top-tier First Division in 1909 after its first season in the league.

9. the Spurs were relegated and promoted a few times until 1950. They won the Second Division crown in 1949-50 and followed up with their first-ever First Division title the very next season. A decade later, in 1960-61, the side won the First Division and the FA Cup for the first such "Double" since Aston Villa pulled it off in 1896-97.

10. Tottenham won the European Cup Winners' Cup in 1962-63 to become the first British outfit to hoist a major European trophy. By 1973-74, they had also become the first English team to reach three major European competition finals and, in 1985, the team colors were changed to white shirts and white shorts. However, just two years later, the kit returns to white shirts and navy-blue shorts.

CHAPTER 2:

THE CAPTAIN CLASS

QUIZ TIME!

1. Who was the club's first captain?

    a. Bobby Buckle

    b. Jack Jull

    c. Jack L. Jones

    d. Sandy Tait

2. Tottenham alternated captains each month during the 2009-10 season.

    a. True

    b. False

3. Which player did Hugo Lloris succeed as skipper?

    a. Ledley King

    b. Michael Dawson

    c. Younès Kaboul

    d. Harry Kane

4. Richard Gough captained which club to nine league titles after leaving Tottenham.

    a. Dundee United
    b. Aberdeen FC
    c. Rangers FC
    d. Charlton Athletic

5. Who captained the side during its first season in the Premier League?

    a. Gary Mabbutt
    b. Sol Campbell
    c. Teddy Sheringham
    d. Billy Minter

6. Which club did Dave Mackay captain before joining Tottenham?

    a. Fulham FC
    b. Preston North End
    c. Sunderland AFC
    d. Heart of Midlothian

7. Jan Vertonghen was the team's first skipper born outside the British Isles.

    a. True
    b. False

8. Garry Mabbutt succeeded which player as captain?

    a. Alan Mullery
    b. Martin Peters

c. Richard Gough

d. Stephen Clemence

9. Which club did Jamie Redknapp wear the armband with before joining Tottenham?

a. Liverpool FC

b. Southampton FC

c. Manchester City

d. Crystal Palace

10. Which player captained the club to its first FA Cup?

a. Arthur Grimsdell

b. Walter Bull

c. Sandy Tait

d. Jack L. Jones

11. Sol Campbell captained which club after leaving Tottenham?

a. Everton FC

b. Queens Park Rangers

c. Aston Villa

d. Portsmouth FC

12. Steve Perryman captained the Spurs to their first international trophy.

a. True

b. False

13. Who lifted the League Cup in 2007-08?

a. Darren Bent

b. Dimitar Berbatov

c. Ledley King

d. Aaron Lennon

14. Who succeeded Garry Mabbutt as skipper?

    a. Cecil Poynton

    b. Jamie Redknapp

    c. Teddy Sheringham

    d. Sol Campbell

15. Which skipper went on to manage the England national men's team?

    a. Michael Dawson

    b. Bobby Smith

    c. Sir Alf Ramsey

    d. John Ryden

16. Ron Burgess captained the Spurs to their first First Division title.

    a. True

    b. False

17. Who wore the armband between 2012 and 2014?

    a. Michael Dawson

    b. Jamie Redknapp

    c. Ledley King

    d. Teddy Sheringham

18. Which skipper played all outfield positions for the club and was once the emergency goalkeeper against Coventry?

    a. Tony Marchi

    b. Martin Peters

c. Willie Hall

d. Les Howe

19. Which skipper scored 13 goals in 15 games for England?

   a. Ron Burgess

   b. Bobby Smith

   c. Alf Ramsey

   d. Danny Blanchflower

20. In 1998 Sol Campbell became England's second-youngest senior national team captain.

   a. True

   b. False

QUIZ ANSWERS

1. A – Bobby Buckle

2. B – False

3. C – Younès Kaboul

4. C – Rangers FC

5. A – Gary Mabbutt

6. D – Heart of Midlothian

7. B – False

8. C – Richard Gough

9. A – Liverpool FC

10. D – Jack L. Jones

11. D – Portsmouth FC

12. B – False

13. C – Ledley King

14. D – Sol Campbell

15. C – Sir Alf Ramsey

16. A – True

17. A – Michael Dawson

18. D – Les Howe

19. B – Bobby Smith

20. A – True

DID YOU KNOW?

1. It's believed that the Spurs have had approximately 37 full-time captains between 1882 and 2021. The first was Bobby Buckle and the most recent is French international goalkeeper Hugo Lloris. Just two of the skippers have hailed from outside of the British Isles. The first was French international defender Younès Kaboul in 2007-08 followed by Lloris in 2015.

2. Younès Kaboul signed in July 2007 from A.J. Auxerre and quickly became a fan favorite due to his on-pitch aggression. He fell out of favor with manager Juande Ramos, but still helped the side win the 2007-08 League Cup. He suffered an injury shortly afterward, which sidelined him for the season. Kaboul publicly criticized Ramos for his lack of playing time when healthy and left in the summer of 2008 for Portsmouth. Kaboul returned from Portsmouth in January 2010 and was given the armband in September 2014. He then joined Sunderland in July 2015.

3. Bobby Buckle, who was one of the original 11 schoolboys who helped form the club in 1882, was elected as the side's first skipper just before turning 14 years old. Buckle is believed to have scored the team's first recorded goal on Oct. 20, 1883. He carried out several jobs with the club early in its history and was appointed its honorary

secretary and treasurer in 1890. Buckle was elected to the first board of directors in 1898 but resigned in 1900. As a player, it's believed he netted 25 goals in 53 official games from 1882 to 1895.

4. Tottenham fans will always have a soft spot in their hearts for Ledley King because he played 323 times between 1999 and 2012 and chipped in with 14 goals after spending his youth career at the club. The English international suffered several injuries during his career and retired at the age of 31. The club captain from 2005 to 2012, he lifted the League Cup in 2007-08 and helped the side reach the European Champions League for the first time in 2010-11. King once scored a Premier League goal after just 9.82 seconds at Bradford City to set a record for the fastest league goal at the time. He remained with the club as an ambassador and recently joined the coaching staff.

5. Defender and midfielder Steve Perryman played with the Spurs from 1969 to 1986 and wore the armband for the last 11 years of his stint. He was named the FWA Footballer of the Year for 1982 and holds the club record with 854 overall appearances and 655 league games while chipping in with 39 goals. He helped the squad win two FA and League Cups, along with two UEFA Cups. He joined as a schoolboy and eventually joined Oxford as a player-coach in 1986, Perryman returned in 1993 as an assistant manager and served as caretaker boss for a spell in 1994.

6. The first long-term captain of the club was John "Jack" Jones, a Welsh international forward and amateur cricket player. He joined Tottenham in May 1897 from Sheffield United for free and remained until joining Watford in 1904. Jones captained the side to the 1900-01 FA Cup by beating his former team, Sheffield United. After hanging up his boots, he coached Bohemian FC in Ireland before moving to South Africa. He later returned to England to coach the Whitburn Cricket Club.

7. Ron Burgess was a Welsh international midfielder who kicked off his career with the Spurs from 1938 to 1954. His early career was interrupted by World War II but, when the league returned to normal in 1946, he was named team captain and became a key player. He skippered the side to the 1950-51 First Division title just a season after leading it to the Second Division crown and he also wore the armband for his homeland. Burgess joined Swansea Town in 1954 and later managed the club. His nephew, Clive Burgess, was an international rugby union player for the Welsh team from 1977 to 1982.

8. English international defender Gary Mabbutt played with Tottenham from 1982 until 1998 and wore the armband between 1987 and 1998. He joined from Bristol Rovers and helped his teammates capture a UEFA Cup and FA Cup. He suffered a fractured skull and eye socket in 1993 and a broken leg in 1996 before retiring in 1998. Mabbutt played 611 games with the team to rank second on the Spurs' all-time appearance list. In 2018, a rat ate part of Mabbutt's

foot while he was on holiday in Kruger National Park in South Africa.

9. The first Scottish-born Spurs skipper was Alexander "Sandy" Tait, from 1904 to 1907. The defender was one of 13 children and joined from Preston North End in1899 while the Spurs were in the Southern League. Known as "Terrible Tait" because of his tough tackling, he helped the team win the 1899-1900 Southern League and the 1900-01 FA Cup. He spent eight seasons with the club and played approximately 350 games. Tait joined Leyton in 1908 and later became a football manager.

10. Sir Alf Ramsey is famous for playing with England and managing the team to the 1966 World Cup, but he was also a fine player. He joined Tottenham from Southampton in 1949 and played until retiring in 1955. He was an England captain and also skippered the Spurs between 1954 and 1955. The defender was on the side that won the Second Division title in 1949-50 and the First Division crown in 1950-51 and played 250 times for the team. Ramsey was inducted into the English Football Hall of Fame in 2002.

CHAPTER 3:

AMAZING MANAGERS

QUIZ TIME!

1. Who was the club's first manager?

    a. Peter McWilliam

    b. Fred Kirkham

    c. John Cameron

    d. Frank Brettell

2. Tottenham has had 50 different full-time managers as of 2020.

    a. True

    b. False

3. Which manager did José Mourinho succeed?

    a. André Villas-Boas

    b. Harry Redknapp

    c. Tim Sherwood

    d. Mauricio Pochettino

4. Which club did Harry Redknapp manage after leaving Tottenham?

    a. West Ham United
    b. AFC Bournemouth
    c. Queens Park Rangers
    d. Portsmouth FC

5. Juande Ramos succeeded which Spurs' boss?

    a. Martin Jol
    b. Jacques Santini
    c. David Pleat
    d. Glenn Hoddle

6. Who was the club's first manager born outside of the British Isles?

    a. Martin Jol
    b. Jacques Santini
    c. Osvaldo Ardiles
    d. Christian Gross

7. Mauricio Pochettino won over 200 games with Tottenham.

    a. True
    b. False

8. Who succeeded Terry Venables as manager?

    a. Joe Hulme
    b. Arthur Turner
    c. Doug Livermore
    d. Peter Shreeves

9. Who served as club manager the longest?

    a. Harry Redknapp
    b. Terry Neill
    c. Peter McWilliam
    d. Gerry Francis

10. Jacques Santini managed which club after he left Tottenham?

    a. AS Saint-Étienne
    b. Olympique Lyon
    c. A.J. Auxerre
    d. Lille OSC

11. Which manager succeeded Bill Nicholson?

    a. Jimmy Anderson
    b. Peter Shreeves
    c. Keith Burkinshaw
    d. Terry Neill

12. Tottenham was the first club Christian Gross ever managed.

    a. True
    b. False

13. Including the FA Charity Shield, how many trophies did Bill Nicholson win as manager?

    a. 10
    b. 11
    c. 7
    d. 4

14. Who was the first Spurs boss to win the Premier League Manager of the Season award?

    a. André Villas-Boas
    b. Gerry Francis
    c. George Graham
    d. Harry Redknapp

15. José Mourinho left which club to join Tottenham as manager?

    a. S.S. Lazio
    b. Manchester United
    c. Real Madrid
    d. Manchester City

16. Doug Livermore and Ray Clemence were joint managers in Tottenham's first season in the Premier League.

    a. True
    b. False

17. Where was Osvaldo Ardiles born?

    a. Argentina
    b. Peru
    c. Bolivia
    d. Chile

18. Which manager signed Gareth Bale?

    a. George Graham
    b. David Pleat
    c. Steve Perryman
    d. Martin Jol

19. Juande Ramos left which club to manage Tottenham>

   a. Valencia CF
   b. FC Barcelona
   c. Sevilla FC
   d. Real Madrid

20. As of 2020, seven different Spurs' managers have won the Premier League Manager of the Season award.

   a. True
   b. False

QUIZ ANSWERS

1. D – Frank Brettell

2. B – False

3. D – Mauricio Pochettino

4. C – Queens Park Rangers

5. A – Marin Jol

6. C – Osvaldo Ardiles

7. B – False

8. D – Peter Shreeves

9. C – Peter McWilliam

10. C – A.J. Auxerre

11. D – Terry Neill

12. B – False

13. B – 11

14. D – Harry Redknapp

15. B – Manchester United

16. A – True

17. A – Argentina

18. D – Martin Jol

19. C – Sevilla FC

20. B – False

DID YOU KNOW?

1. The Spurs have had approximately 40 different managers at the club either in a full-time or caretaker capacity since 1898. Frank Brettell is listed as the first from 1898 to 1899 and José Mourinho was the current boss as of March 2021, after being appointed on Nov. 20, 2019. In addition, directors ran the team between 1908 and 1913, with Arthur Turner recognized by some club historians as being in charge during this time.

2. Frank Brettell was the team's first boss but was in charge for just one season. The former Everton player was the secretary of Bolton Wanderers in 1898 when he joined the Spurs and left for Portsmouth a year later. It's believed that Brettell was in charge of the club for 63 games and won 37 of them. This would make him the full-time manager with the best winning percentage at the club at 58.73 percent.

3. John Cameron was signed in 1898 as a player by manager Frank Brettell and became player-manager of the Spurs when Brettell left a year later. He led the team to the Southern Football League title in 1899-1900 and the next season he helped it win the FA Cup in a replay against Sheffield United. The first game had ended 2-2 but Tottenham won the second outing 3-1 and Cameron netted

the opening goal. Cameron resigned as manager in March 1907.

4. After being named secretary of Tottenham in 1906, Arthur Turner basically ran the team between 1908 and 1910 for the club directors. He took over as official manager many years later, in August 1942, when the Football League suspended play due to World War II. The team played friendlies during this period and, when the war was over, Turner was replaced as manager by Joe Hulme. Turner remained with the club until passing away in 1949 after 43 years with the Spurs.

5. The first manager to hail from outside of the British Isles was former Spurs' player Osvaldo "Ossie" Ardiles of Argentina in 1993. Following Ardiles, other non-British or Irish bosses appointed were Christian Gross of Switzerland (1997), Jacques Santini of France (2004), Martin Jol of Holland (2004), Juande Ramos of Spain (2007), André Villas-Boas of Portugal (2012), Mauricio Pochettino of Argentina (2014), and José Mourinho of Portugal in 2019.

6. Bill Nicholson played with the side from 1938 to 1955 and managed it from 1958 to 1974 to become the Spurs' longest-serving consecutive, and most successful boss. He was associated with the outfit for 36 years and guided the side to eight major trophies during his 16-year managerial stint. As a player, he won a First and Second Division title, as well as the 1951 FA Charity Shield. As a manager, he won three FA Cups, three FA Charity Shields, two League

Cups, a UEFA Cup, a European Cup Winners' Cup, and a First Division title.

7. Peter McWilliam of Scotland managed the Spurs from 1913 to 1927 and again from 1938 to 1942 to rank as the longest-serving manager in total years. However, World War I interrupted his first stint and World War II his second spell. The former Scottish international played for Inverness and Newcastle United before taking over the reins at Tottenham. Known as "Peter the Great," he helped the side win the Second Division title in 1919-20, the FA Cup in 1920-21, and the FA Charity Shield in 1921. He joined Middlesbrough as manager in 1927 and returned to Tottenham in 1938.

8. Martin Jol didn't win any silverware with Tottenham Hotspur and won just under 45 percent of his games as the team's manager between 2004 and 2007. However, the Dutchman came close to earning a European Champions League spot in 2005-06, but the side was narrowly beaten by arch-rivals Arsenal, for fourth place in the Premier League. He did take the side to the Europa League and signed striker Dimitar Berbatov as well as Gareth Bale.

9. After hanging up his boots, Keith Burkinshaw moved to Zambia to coach and then took over as manager of Newcastle United. However, he was fired in May 1975 and joined Tottenham a year later to replace Terry Neill, who had left for Arsenal. Burkinshaw held the Spurs' job until May 1984, winning two straight FA Cups, a UEFA

Cup, and an FA Charity Shield. His rein was rocky to begin with, as the team was relegated after his first season but was promoted the following campaign. The team won the 1983-84 UEFA Cup in his final game in charge.

10. Former Spurs player Harry Redknapp was appointed manager in October 2008, after Juande Ramos was fired with the club, sitting in last place in the Premier League. He led the side to an eighth place finish, and they reached the 2008-09 League Cup final, only to lose in a penalty shootout against Manchester United. The next season the club finished fourth in the league to qualify for the European Champions League, and Redknapp was named the Premier League Manager of the Year. However, after another fourth-place finish, he was fired in June 2012.

CHAPTER 4:

GOALTENDING GREATS

QUIZ TIME!

1. Which keeper made the most appearances for Tottenham?

    a. Ian Walker
    b. Ted Ditchburn
    c. Pat Jennings
    d. Bill Brown

2. Hugo Lloris was born in Belgium but plays nationally for France.

    a. True
    b. False

3. Which keeper made 13 appearances behind Paul Robinson in the 2007-08 domestic league?

    a. Heurelho Gomes
    b. Kasey Keller
    c. Carlo Cudicini
    d. Radek Černý

4. How many clean sheets did Hugo Lloris keep in the 2017-18 Premier League?

    a. 27

    b. 22

    c. 15

    d. 11

5. Which club did Brad Friedel leave to join Tottenham?

    a. Everton FC

    b. Aston Villa

    c. Queens Park Rangers

    d. Newcastle United

6. How many appearances did Heurelho Gomes make in the 2009-10 domestic league?

    a. 17

    b. 35

    c. 27

    d. 31

7. Pat Jennings won the FWA Footballer of the Year award in 1972-73.

    a. True

    b. False

8. Who made 18 appearances behind Hugo Lloris in the 2019-20 Premier League?

    a. Paulo Gazzaniga

    b. Michael Vorm

c. Pau López

d. Like McGee

9. How many clean sheets did Brad Friedel keep in the 2011-12 Premier League?

   a. 20

   b. 17

   c. 14

   d. 10

10. Which keeper played in the Spurs' first-ever Premier League match?

    a. Bobby Mimms

    b. Kevin Dearden

    c. Ian Walker

    d. Erik Thorstvedt

11. Paul Watson left what club to join Tottenham?

    a. Wolverhampton Wanders

    b. Leeds United

    c. Blackburn Rovers

    d. Bolton Wanderers

12. Hugo Lloris won the FIFA Best Goalkeeper award in 2018.

    a. True

    b. False

13. From which club did Kasey Keller join Tottenham?

    a. Fulham FC

    b. Borussia Mönchengladbach

c. Seattle Sounders FC

d. Southampton FC

14. Who made 35 appearances in the 2000-01 Premier League?

a. Neil Sullivan

b. Ian Walker

c. Kasey Keller

d. Espen Baardsen

15. How many games did Pat Jennings make in all competitions for the team?

a. 564

b. 571

c. 590

d. 613

16. Tony Parks played in less than 40 league matches in seven seasons with the club.

a. True

b. False

17. How many appearances did Pat Jennings make for the Irish national team while with Tottenham?

a. 53

b. 64

c. 71

d. 88

18. Who backed up Ian Walker for 12 games in the 1998-99 Premier League?

    a. Neil Sullivan
    b. Espen Baardsen
    c. Hans Segers
    d. Erik Thorstvedt

19. How many appearances did Ted Ditchburn make in all competitions for Tottenham?

    a. 408
    b. 452
    c. 544
    d. 580

20. Ian Walker was promoted from Tottenham's youth system.

    a. True
    b. False

QUIZ ANSWERS

1. C – Pat Jennings

2. B – False

3. D – Radek Černý

4. C – 15

5. B – Aston Villa

6. D – 31

7. A – True

8. A – Paulo Gazzaniga

9. C – 14

10. D – Erik Thorstvedt

11. B – Leeds United

12. B – False

13. D – Southampton FC

14. A – Neil Sullivan

15. C – 590

16. A – True

17. C – 71

18. B – Espen Baardsen

19. B – 452

20. A – True

DID YOU KNOW?

1. One of the club's first keepers was Charles Ambler, who had two spells with Tottenham. He turned pro with Royal Arsenal but returned to amateur football before signing with the Spurs in October 1894. However, since the club wasn't competing in an organized league at the time, Ambler also played with other teams, including Woolwich Arsenal. He returned to Tottenham from 1896 to 1900 and played 22 Southern League matches. He played just over 130 games with the side before joining West Ham United.

2. American international Brad Friedel played 84 times for his homeland to set the record for goalkeepers and appeared in three World Cups. He made a name for himself in the Premier League with Liverpool, Blackburn, and Aston Villa before joining the Spurs in 2011. As of 2020, Friedel held the Premier League record for the most consecutive matches played at 310. That streak ended when he was left out of the Spurs' squad on Oct. 7, 2012. On May 6, 2012, he became the club's oldest competitive player when he guarded the goal in a Premier League outing at Aston Villa.

3. Another American international great to play in goal with Tottenham was Kasey Keller, who joined from Rayo Vallecano in 2001 on a free transfer. He started at White Hart Lane as backup to Neil Sullivan but played every

minute for the team in the 2002-03 and the 2003-04 campaigns. He fell out of favor in the 2004-05 Premier League season as Paul Robinson took over as the number one. Keller was loaned to Southampton in November 2004 for a month when that club had an injury crisis in goal. He then joined Borussia Mönchengladbach on a free transfer in January 2005.

4. The first American-born keeper to try his luck with the club was Espen Baardsen, whose parents hailed from Norway. He played for the USA under-18 national team before switching his international eligibility to Norway, and he played four times with the national senior team. He was offered a contract by the Spurs while playing in San Francisco and made his English debut in 1997 against Liverpool at Anfield. He won a League Cup winners medal in 1998-99 but realized he would be relegated to a backup role with the team. Baardsen then signed with Watford for a reported £1.25 million in 2000 and he retired in 2002 at the age of 25.

5. Northern Ireland international Pat Jennings played a goalkeeper record-high 590 games for the Spurs, including 472 league matches. He joined from Watford in 1964 and left for Arsenal in 1977. He returned to Tottenham for the 1985-86 campaign, and then joined Everton. Jennings won an FA Cup, two League Cups, and a UEFA Cup and scored a goal in the 1967 FA Charity Shield to help the Spurs down Manchester United. Jennings was named the Football Writers' Association

(FWA) Player of the Year in 1972-73 and the PFA's Player of the Year in 1975-76 to become the first keeper to win the honor. He was also named to the PFA First Division Team of the Year for 1973-74 and 1975-76 and was inducted into the English Football Hall of Fame in 2003.

6. Ray Clemence was an English international who joined the Spurs from Liverpool in August 1981 when he was 33 years old. He played 330 times before a knee injury forced him to retire in March 1988. Clemence helped the side share the 1981 FA Charity Shield and win the 1981-82 FA Cup in his first season but was injured for the UEFA Cup triumph in 1983-84 and sat on the substitute's bench. His final match came against Norwich City in October 1987, which was his 1,119th first-class career appearance. Clemence later became the Spurs' goalkeeping coach, reserve team manager, and assistant manager at White Hart Lane.

7. Dutch international Michel Vorm joined Tottenham for a reported £3.5 million in July 2014 from Swansea City and retired in 2020. He arrived to provide competition for Hugo Lloris shortly after Mauricio Pochettino took over as manager and went on to play 47 times, including the Premier League, European Champions League, and semi-finals in both the League and FA Cups. Vorm also played 15 national games for his homeland. The Spurs released him after the 2018-19 campaign but re-signed him a few months later when Lloris was sidelined with an injury.

8. Tony Parks played with over 15 clubs in his 20-plus year pro career but started with Tottenham between 1981-82 and 1987-88, spending parts of his final two seasons on loan. Although he was never a regular starter with the side, Parks was the hero of the 1983-84 UEFA Cup final when the Spurs beat defending champions Anderlecht in a penalty shootout. He made two saves in the shootout to secure the victory and left the club in 1988 to join Brentford. Parks returned to the Spurs years later as a goalkeeping coach.

9. After spending his youth career with Tottenham, Ian Walker spent time with Oxford United and Ipswich Town before becoming a regular with the Spurs in 1991-92. He played over 300 games with the team before joining Leicester City in 2001 and posted a clean sheet in a 1-0 victory over Leicester in the 1998-99 League Cup final. Walker eventually lost his place to Neil Sullivan and then asked to be transferred. He played four times for England and later moved to China to work as a goalkeeping coach.

10. Even though Paul Robinson played 41 times for England, he remains one of his country's most underrated keepers. He joined the Spurs from Leeds United in 2004 and proceeded to play 112 of the team's next 114 Premier League matches over the next three seasons. Robinson scored the second goal of his pro career against Watford at home in March 2007 and wore the captain's armband on occasion. He played 25 league games in 2007-08 as Radek Černý provided him with competition but was in

goal for their League Cup final triumph. Robinson played 175 games before joining Blackburn Rovers in July 2008 for a reported £3.5 million.

CHAPTER 5:

DARING DEFENDERS

QUIZ TIME!

1. Who made the most appearances for the club?

    a. Gary Mabbutt

    b. Cyril Knowles

    c. Thomas Clay

    d. Chris Hughton

2. Jan Vertonghen made 80 appearances for the Belgian men's national team while playing for Tottenham.

    a. True

    b. False

3. How many goals did Sol Campbell score in all competitions with Tottenham?

    a. 19

    b. 9

    c. 22

    d. 15

4. Which club did Gary Mabbutt leave to join Tottenham?

    a. Swindon Town
    b. Bristol Rovers FC
    c. Fulham FC
    d. Sunderland AFC

5. Which player made 50 appearances in all competitions in 2018-19?

    a. Ben Davies
    b. Davinson Sánchez
    c. Toby Alderweireld
    d. Eric Dier

6. How many goals did Gary Mabbutt score for the team in all competitions?

    a. 18
    b. 29
    c. 38
    d. 44

7. Serge Aurier was shown 10 yellow cards in the 2019-20 Premier League.

    a. True
    b. False

8. From which club did Michael Dawson join Tottenham?

    a. Newcastle United
    b. Hull City FC
    c. Sheffield United
    d. Nottingham Forest

9. Which player was shown a red card in the 2005-06 Premier League?

   a. Paul Stalteri
   b. Young-pyo Lee
   c. Ledley King
   d. Anthony Gardener

10. How many appearances did Thomas Clay make in all competitions for the Spurs?

   a. 309
   b. 324
   c. 351
   d. 377

11. Which player scored 3 goals in the 1992-93 Premier League season?

   a. Jason Cundy
   b. Sol Campbell
   c. Gary Mabbutt
   d. Neil Ruddock

12. Michael Dawson won the FWA Footballer of the Year award in 2012-13.

   a. True
   b. False

13. From which Scottish club did Alan Hutton join Tottenham?

   a. Hamilton Academical FC
   b. Rangers FC

c. Dundee United

d. Celtic FC

14. Which player appeared in 36 matches in the 2012-13 Premier League?

    a. Kyle Walker

    b. Jan Vertonghen

    c. William Gallas

    d. Steven Caulker

15. How many appearances did Gary Mabbutt make in all competitions?

    a. 475

    b. 523

    c. 558

    d. 611

16. Benoît Assou-Ekotto was shown 11 yellow cards in all competitions in 2009-10.

    a. True

    b. False

17. Which player tallied 5 assists in the 2007-08 domestic league?

    a. Michael Dawson

    b. Young-pyo Lee

    c. Pascal Chimbonda

    d. Younès Kaboul

18. How many appearances did Cyril Knowles make in all competitions?

a. 422

b. 506

c. 541

d. 570

19. Which player scored 3 goals in the 2014-15 Premier League?

a. Paulinho

b. Federico Fazio

c. Eric Dier

d. Danny Rose

20. William Gallas tallied 7 assists in all competitions in 2010-11.

a. True

b. False

QUIZ ANSWERS

1. A – Gary Mabbutt

2. A – True

3. D – 15

4. B – Bristol Rovers FC

5. C – Toby Alderweireld

6. C – 38

7. B – False

8. D – Nottingham Forest

9. A – Paul Stalteri

10. C – 351

11. D – Neil Ruddock

12. B – False

13. B – Rangers FC

14. A – Kyle Walker

15. D – 611

16. B – False

17. C – Pascal Chimbonda

18. B – 506

19. D – Danny Rose

20. B – False

DID YOU KNOW?

1. Henry "Harry" Clarke spent his entire senior career at Tottenham and played once with England. He arrived in March 1949 from Lovell's Athletic and played over 300 games until retiring in December 1956. He helped the team win the Second Division in 1949-50 and played all 42 games in the 1950-51 league when the Spurs captured the First Division. The powerful Clarke was dominant in the air and helped coach the team after hanging up his boots for the last time.

2. A powerhouse defender, Maurice Norman played 411 games after joining from Norwich City in 1955. The England international won the Second Division in 1949-50 and the First Division the next season and played 48 of 49 games in 1960-61, when the team won the First Division and FA Cup double. He also won the FA Cup in 1961-62 and the European Cup Winners' Cup in 1962-1963. Unfortunately, in November 1965, he suffered a serious leg injury that basically ended his career.

3. Republic of Ireland international Chris Hughton played two games short of 400 in his Tottenham stint, which ran from 1977 to 1990 which jump-started his career. Joining as a youth, the English-born Hughton started as a winger before moving to the back line. He was a member of the side that captured the FA Cup in 1980-81 and 1981-82, as

well as the 1983-84 UEFA Cup. Hughton also won a runners-up FA Cup and League Cup medal before joining West Ham United in November 1990 on loan, and then permanently, on a free transfer. He later became a football manager and had stints as the Spurs' caretaker boss.

4. Mike England joined Tottenham from Blackburn Rovers in 1966 and helped the side win the FA Cup in his first season. The Welsh international was vital in defense and played 397 times for the squad before heading for America in 1975 to join the Seattle Sounders. He also helped the team win two League Cups and a UEFA Cup. He played 44 times for his homeland and was his country's youngest permanent captain until Aaron Ramsey broke the mark in 2011. England later managed the Wales national team between 1980 and 1988.

5. Phil Beal joined as a youth in 1960 and signed as a pro two years later, making his debut in 1963. He missed the 1966-67 FA Cup final win over Chelsea, due to a broken arm, but helped the side win the League Cup in 1970-1971 and 1972-73, as well as the 1971-72 UEFA Cup. Beal left White Hart Lane in 1975 to join Brighton and Hove Albion and later played in America before returning to England. After retiring, he became a match-day host with Tottenham.

6. Central defender Graham Roberts joined the Spurs in 1980 from non-league Weymouth and stayed until 1986 when he joined Glasgow Rangers in Scotland. He could

also play in the midfield if needed and helped his teammates hoist two straight FA Cups, in 1980-81 and 1981-82, and share the 1981 FA Charity Shield. Roberts also helped them capture the 1983-84 UEFA Cup by scoring in the second leg against Anderlecht. The England international appeared in over 200 games with Tottenham and entered football management after retiring.

7. Paul Miller also developed in Tottenham's youth ranks before spending a season in Norway to gain experience. He went on to play nearly300 games with the club between 1977 and 1987. The central defender went about his business, with little fanfare, and helped the side share the 1981 FA Charity Shield, as well as win two FA Cups and a UEFA Cup. He scored against Anderlecht in the first leg of the UEFA Cup final. Miller left after a decade when he joined Charlton Athletic.

8. Scottish international Richard Gough played fewer than 70 games with the club after joining from Dundee United, in the summer of 1986 for a reported £750,000, but had a major impact on his teammates. He captained the team to the 1986-87 FA Cup final, where they were beaten 3-2 in extra time by Coventry City. Gough decided to return to Scotland early in the 1987-88 campaign and was transferred to Glasgow Rangers. This saw him become the first Sottish player to be bought by a Scottish club for more than £1 million. Gough later played in America before hanging up his boots.

9. Although Cyril Knowles played just four times for England, he appeared in 506 matches with the Spurs between 1964 and 1974, and as a stalwart of the Spurs first team, missed just one league contest between 1965 and 1969. He joined from Middlesbrough in May 1964 and won the 1966-67 FA Cup, the 1970-71 and 1972-73 League Cups, and the 1971-72 UEFA Cup. He also helped the Spurs draw Manchester United 3-3 in the 1967 FA Charity Shield. Knowles scored just 17 goals but two of them came in a crucial victory over Leeds United to stave off relegation in 1974-75. Knowles inspired the song "Nice One Cyril" by Cockerel Chorus, which reached number 14 in the UK singles chart.

10. Former Spur captain Michael Dawson was well known for giving it his utmost effort on the pitch in every game. The central defender displayed sheer determination when the odds were against him and his teammates, and led by example. He joined in January 2015 from Nottingham Forest, along with winger Andy Reid, and remained until 2018 when he signed with Hull City. He helped the Spurs win the 2007-08 League Cup even though he missed the final against Chelsea. They reached the League Cup final again the next season but lost a penalty shootout to Manchester United. Dawson was named Tottenham Hotspur Player of the Year for 2009-10 and played over 300 games with the team.

CHAPTER 6:

MAESTROS OF THE MIDFIELD

QUIZ TIME!

1. Who made his club debut as a 17-year-old in 1969?

   a. Terry Venables
   b. Steve Perryman
   c. Alan Mullery
   d. Glenn Hoddle

2. Jamie Redknapp was shown 6 yellow cards in the 2003-04 domestic league season.

   a. True
   b. False

3. How many appearances did Mousa Dembélé make for the Belgian men's national team while playing with Tottenham?

   a. 27
   b. 51
   c. 35
   d. 42

4. Who scored 6 goals in the 2013-14 Premier League season?

   a. Mousa Dembélé
   b. Sandro
   c. Paulinho
   d. Lewis Holtby

5. From which club did Luka Modrić join Tottenham?

   a. Dinamo Zagreb
   b. NK Zadar
   c. NK Varaždin
   d. NK Instra 1961

6. Which player appeared in 41 matches in all competitions in 2019-20?

   a. Tanguy Ndombélé
   b. Moussa Sissoko
   c. Giovani Lo Celso
   d. Harry Winks

7. Tom Huddlestone tallied 10 assists in the 2007-08 Premier League.

   a. True
   b. False

8. How many appearances did Glenn Hoddle make in all competitions with the club?

   a. 533
   b. 490

c. 452

d. 415

9. Which player scored 7 goals in all competitions in 2007-08?

   a. Steed Malbranque

   b. Jermaine Jenas

   c. Tom Huddlestone

   d. Jamie O'Hara

10. Which player scored 3 goals in the 1992-93 Premier League?

   a. Andy Turner

   b. Nayim

   c. Paul Allen

   d. Andy Gray

11. How many appearances did Luka Modrić make with the Croatian men's national team while playing with Tottenham?

   a. 30

   b. 21

   c. 14

   d. 8

12. Steve Perryman won the FWA Footballer of the Year award in 1981-82.

   a. True

   b. False

13. Which midfielder left the Spurs to play with Portland Timbers in America?

    a. Scott Parker

    b. John Pratt

    c. Tim Sherwood

    d. Paul Gascoigne

14. Who scored 6 goals in all competitions in 1996-97?

    a. Jason Dozzell

    b. Andy Sinton

    c. Allan Nielsen

    d. David Howells

15. How many appearances did Glenn Hoddle make for the England men's national team while playing with Tottenham?

    a. 16

    b. 27

    c. 35

    d. 44

16. Ossie Ardiles scored 25 goals in all competitions with Tottenham.

    a. True

    b. False

17. Which player made 47 appearances in all competitions in 2017-18?

    a. Moussa Sissoko

    b. Harry Winks

c. Mousa Dembélé

d. Victor Wanyama

18. Who received a three-match ban for elbowing Harry Arter of Bournemouth in October 2016?

a. Victor Wanyama

b. Dele Alli

c. Moussa Sissoko

d. Harry Winks

19. Michael Carrick joined Tottenham from what club?

a. Leeds United

b. Swindon Town FC

c. Blackburn Rovers

d. West Ham United

20. Ryan Mason was the only Spurs player to be shown a red card in the 2015-16 Premier League season.

a. True

b. False

QUIZ ANSWERS

1. B – Steve Perryman

2. A – True

3. D – 42

4. C – Paulinho

5. A – Dinamo Zagreb

6. D – Harry Winks

7. B – False

8. B – 490

9. A – Steed Malbranque

10. C – Paul Allen

11. B – 21

12. A – True

13. B – John Pratt

14. B – Andy Sinton

15. D – 44

16. A – True

17. A – Moussa Sissoko

18. C – Moussa Sissoko

19. D – West Ham United

20. B – False

DID YOU KNOW?

1. Midfield genius Paul "Gazza" Gascoigne notched 33 goals in his 112 games with Tottenham, after arriving from Newcastle United, where he debuted as a 17-year-old and won the 1987-88 PFA Young Player of the Year Award. The English international free spirit brought passion, imagination, and creativity to the pitch and was an excellent taker of free kicks. He helped the team win the 1990-91 FA Cup after scoring a stunning free-kick goal in the semi-final against Arsenal and was named to the PFA First Division Team of the Year in 1990–91. Unfortunately, Gazza suffered a serious knee injury in the final and left for Lazio in Italy in 1992.

2. Belgian international Mousa Dembélé transferred to the Spurs in August 2012, when they paid his reported £15 million release clause from Fulham, and he scored on his debut. In May 2016, he was suspended for six games for allegedly gouging the eye of Chelsea's Diego Costa, even though he wasn't booked by the referee. Dembélé struggled with injuries in 2016-17 and underwent ankle surgery in May 2017. However, he still had problems with his ankle and missed several more games. Dembélé joined Guangzhou City in China in January 2019 after just under 250 appearances.

3. Scottish international Dave Mackay arrived from Heart of Midlothian in 1959 for a reported £32,000 at the age of 24

and contributed just over 50 goals in 318 games before joining Derby County in 1968. Mackay was a key member of the 1960-61 First Division and FA Cup double-winning side. He also helped the team win FA Cups in 1961-62 and 19166-67, the European Cup Winners' Cup in 1962-63, and a trio of FA Charity Shields. Mackay missed 18 months of action after breaking his leg in December, and his absence was sorely felt by the team and fans. He later became a prominent football manager.

4. English international Alan Mullery joined Tottenham from Fulham in 1964 and played 373 times for the team before heading back to Fulham eight years later. He helped the squad capture the 1966-67 FA Cup, the 1970-71 League Cup, and the 1971-72 UEFA Cup, scoring the winner in the latter championship. In a 1968 European Championship game against Yugoslavia, Mullery became the first English international player to be sent off in a game when he received a red card. The defensive midfielder retired in 1976 and entered the world of football management.

5. One of Allan Mullery's England teammates was fellow midfielder Martin Peters. He was signed from West Ham United in 1970 for a reported £200,000, with striker Jimmy Greaves leaving the Spurs for West Ham in the transaction. Peters scored on his Tottenham debut and helped the side win the 1970-71 League Cup final and 1971 Anglo-Italian League Cup. He then won the 1971-72 UEFA Cup and 1972-73 League Cup and took home a runners-up medal from the 1973-74 UEFA Cup final.

Peters joined Norwich City in March 1975 after scoring 76 goals in 260 outings with the Spurs. He was elected to the English Football Hall of Fame in 2006.

6. Bamidele "Dele" Alli joined the club from his hometown Milton Keynes Dons team in February 2015 and was loaned back to the Dons for the rest of the season. He made his Spurs' debut six months later and shortly after that played his first senior match for England. Alli won the BBC Goal of the Season Award in 2015-16, as well as the PFA Young Player of the Year Trophy for 2015-16 and 2016-17, and was also named to the PFA Premier League Team of the Year both those seasons. He won a European Champions League runners-up medal in 2018-19 and was still with the club in March 2021. He scored 65 goals in his first 242 appearances.

7. Glenn Hoddle starred with the Spurs from 1975 to 1987 after spending his youth at White Hart Lane. The classy English international appeared in 490 games and scored 110 goals. He made his debut at the age of 17 and won the PFA Young Player of the Year Award for 1979-80. He won two FA Cups and a UEFA Cup while being named to six PFA Teams of the Year before joining Monaco. Hoddle later managed both the Spurs and England, became a TV pundit, and was inducted into the English Football Hall of Fame. He and Spurs' teammate Chris Waddle released a song named "Diamond Lights" in 1987, which peaked at number 12 in the UK singles chart. Hoddle also appeared

on *The Masked Singer* TV show in 2021 and finished in ninth place.

8. Another hugely skilled playmaker who went on to manage the Spurs was Argentine international Ossie Ardiles. He was just 5-feet, 7-inches in height, but was still a giant in the midfield. Ardiles arrived from his homeland in 1978 and remained for a decade until joining Blackburn Rovers. However, when the Falklands War between Britain and Argentina broke out in 1982, he was loaned to Paris Saint-Germain for most of the 1982-83 season. He helped the side win two FA Cups and UEFA Cup and shared the 1981 FA Charity Shield. Ardiles played just over 300 games and notched 25 goals with the Spurs and was named to the PFA First Division Team of the Year for 1978-79.

9. Joining Ossie Ardiles on his journey to Tottenham in 1978 was fellow Argentine international Ricky Villa, who scored on his debut to quickly become a fan favorite and cult hero. He tallied 25 goals in 179 games and one of them being the winner in the 1980-81 FA Cup final replay against Manchester City. Villa's goal was so remarkable it was named the winner of the Wembley Goal of the Century Award in 2001. He helped the side win the FA Cup again the next season before leaving to play in America. Like Ardiles, Villa is a member of the Tottenham Hotspur Hall of Fame.

10. Jermaine Jenas made his pro debut at the age of 17 for Nottingham Forest in the second tier before joining Newcastle United a year later in 2002 for a reported £5 million. He was just 19 when he earned the first of his 21 caps for England and was the PFA Young Player of the Year for 2002-03. Jenas joined Tottenham in 2005 for a reported £7 million and helped the side win the League Cup in 2007-08. He was loaned to Aston Villa in 2011 and Nottingham Forest in 2012 for spells, before joining Queens Park Rangers in January 2013. Jenas played his last games in 2014 due to a serious knee injury and then became a television football pundit. He played just over 200 games with the Spurs and tallied 26 goals.

CHAPTER 7:

SENSATIONAL STRIKERS/FORWARDS

QUIZ TIME!

1. Which player made the most career appearances for Tottenham?

    a. Jimmy Greaves

    b. Martin Chivers

    c. Alan Gilzean

    d. Robbie Keane

2. Harry Kane has received more England caps than any other Spurs player.

    a. True

    b. False

3. Which player scored 11 goals in the 2005-06 Premier League?

    a. Jermaine Defoe

    b. Danny Murphy

    c. Mido

    d. Wayne Routledge

4. Which club did Son Heung-min leave to join the Spurs?

    a. Everton FC
    b. AC Milan
    c. FC Seoul
    d. Bayer Leverkusen

5. Which player scored 7 goals in the 2003-04 Premier League season?

    a. Gustav Poyet
    b. Frédéric Kanouté
    c. Hélder Postiga
    d. Bobby Zamora

6. Which player appeared in 50 matches in all competitions in 2016-17?

    a. Marcus Edwards
    b. Josh Onomah
    c. Dele Alli
    d. Christian Eriksen

7. Gareth Bale won the PFA Players' Player of the Year award twice with Tottenham as of 2020.

    a. True
    b. False

8. Emmanuel Adebayor left which club to join Tottenham?

    a. Liverpool FC
    b. Manchester United
    c. Chelsea FC
    d. Manchester City FC

9. How many appearances did Martin Chivers make for the Spurs in all competitions?

   a. 343
   b. 367
   c. 412
   d. 435

10. Which player made 47 appearances in all competitions in 2019-20?

   a. Lucas Moura
   b. Christian Eriksen
   c. Harry Kane
   d. Dele Alli

11. Jermaine Defoe left which club to begin his first stint with Tottenham?

   a. West Ham United
   b. Toronto FC
   c. Rangers FC
   d. Southampton FC

12. Harry Kane netted 41 goals in all competitions in 2017-18.

   a. True
   b. False

13. How many career appearances did Robbie Keane make with the club?

   a. 274
   b. 306

c. 370

d. 412

14. Which player scored 10 goals in the 2010-11 Premier League campaign?

    a. Peter Crouch

    b. Aaron Lennon

    c. Gareth Bale

    d. Roman Pavlyuchenko

15. Which season did Gary Lineker win the FWA Footballer of the Year award with Tottenham?

    a. 1989-90

    b. 1991-92

    c. 1987-88

    d. 1993-94

16. Steffen Iversen tallied 10 goals in the 1996-97 Premier League season.

    a. True

    b. False

17. How many goals did Gareth Bale score in the 2011-12 domestic league?

    a. 14

    b. 7

    c. 17

    d. 10

18. How many appearances did Alan Gilzean make in all competitions with the club?

    a. 377
    b. 415
    c. 439
    d. 522

19. Which player scored 15 goals in the 1995-96 domestic league?

    a. Steve Slade
    b. Chris Armstrong
    c. Ruel Fox
    d. Ronny Rosenthal

20. Christian Eriksen led the squad with 9 assists in the 2013-14 Premier League season.

    a. True
    b. False

QUIZ ANSWERS

1. C – Alan Gilzean

2. A – True

3. C – Mido

4. D – Bayer Leverkusen

5. B – Frédéric Kanouté

6. C – Dele Alli

7. A – True

8. D – Manchester City FC

9. B – 367

10. A – Lucas Moura

11. A – West Ham United

12. A – True

13. B – 306

14. D – Roman Pavlyuchenko

15. B – 1991-92

16. B – False

17. D – 10

18. C – 439

19. B – Chris Armstrong

20. A – True

DID YOU KNOW?

1. Walter Tull joined the Spurs as an amateur in 1909 from Clapton, and remained with the side until 1911, when he joined Northampton Town. It's believed he was just the third person of mixed heritage to play in the top tier of the Football League, and the first black to play for the Spurs. He joined the squad on its 1909 tour of Argentina and Uruguay after receiving the maximum £10 signing bonus and £4 per week in wages. Tull also played with the reserve team and made 10 official appearances with the first team with 2 goals scored, and 5 goals in 8 non-first class matches. Tull became the first British-born black combat officer in the British Army and was killed in combat in March 1918 at the age of 29.

2. Jimmy Dimmock was also an early club legend, as he scored the winning goal against Wolverhampton Wanderers in the 1920-21 FA Cup final, when the Spurs won the trophy for the second time. The young winger joined the team in 1919 and helped the side win the Second Division title in his first season. He scored 112 goals in 438 games, with 100 of them coming in 400 league outings. He played three times for England, with his debut in April 1921 when he was 20 years and 125 days old, making him the youngest Spurs player at the time to receive a cap. Dimmock left in 1931 to play for Thames Association FC.

3. Dimitar Berbatov arrived at White Hart Lane in 2006 from Bayer Leverkusen for a reported £10.9 million to become the most expensive Bulgarian player. He notched 46 goals in just over 100 outings and scored after just seven minutes in his home debut. He helped the side win the 2007-08 League Cup and he scored in the final against Chelsea. Berbatov formed a lethal partnership with Robbie Keane from 2006 to 2008 and they combined for 90 goals in two seasons. Berbatov was named the team's Player of the Season for 2006-07 and made the PFA Premier League Team of the Year. However, he joined Manchester United in 2008.

4. South Korean international skipper Son Heung-min joined Tottenham from Bayer Leverkusen in 2015 and in 2019 he became the first Asian player to be nominated for the Ballon d'Or. He was the first Asian player to score more than 50 goals in the Premier League, and as of March 2021, had 66 in the league and 103 in 269 overall appearances with the club. He was named the side's Player of the Year for 2018-19 and 2019-2020. Heung-min was also awarded the Premier League and BBC Goal of the Season for 2019-20, the Tottenham Goal of the Season in 2017-18, 2018-19, and 2019-20, and the team's Goal of the Decade for 2010 to 2019.

5. David Ginola netted 22 goals in his 127 appearances with the Spurts between 1997 and 2000 but contributed much more to the team. He helped the side with the League Cup in 1998-99 and was named the PFA Player of the

Year and the FWA Footballer of the Year that season. The stylish French international arrived from Newcastle United and displayed plenty of pace, strength, and skill on the pitch and scored several spectacular goals to become a fan favorite. Ginola left the Spurs for Aston Villa and later became a TV personality in France. Although his Tottenham career was relatively brief, he was inducted into the club's hall of fame.

6. Robbie Keane was one of the Spurs' finest finishers, with 122 goals in 306 appearances. He signed from Leeds United in 2002 and was known for his dribbling skills, creativity, pace, and leadership qualities. Keane made such an impression with Tottenham that Liverpool paid a reported £20.3 million for him in July 2008. However, just six months later, he returned to the Spurs for a reported £12 million and was made captain. Keane was soon loaned out, though, and joined LA Galaxy in America in 2011. He was named Tottenham's Player of the Year three times and won the 2007-08 League Cup. Keane's 68 goals and 146 national appearances are both Republic of Ireland records.

7. The 1992 Spurs Player of the Year was English international Gary Lineker, who joined from Barcelona in 1989. He notched 80 goals in 138 appearances and won the FA Cup in 1990-91 and shared the FA Charity Shield in 1991. Lineker won the top-tier Golden Boot in his first season with the team with 24 goals and added another 28 league goals two seasons later when he was named the

FWA Footballer of the Year for the second time. Lineker moved to Japan in 1991 to continue his career and retired in 1994 with numerous individual and team awards in his cabinet. He's currently a well-known TV pundit in Britain.

8. Another famous football pundit in the UK is Garth Crooks, who tallied 75 goals in 182 outings with the Spurs and added 3 goals in 4 games for England. He joined in 1980 from Stoke City and scored in his debut. Crooks formed an effective striking partnership with Steve Archibald and helped the team win the 1980-81 and 1981-82 FA Cups and the 1983-1984 UEFA Cup. He scored in the 1980-81 FA Cup final. Crooks spent some time on loan with Manchester City in 1983-84 and joined West Bromwich Albion in 1985. In 1988, he became the first black chairman of the Professional Footballers' Association.

9. Clive Allen scored a remarkable 49 goals in 1986-87 to set a Tottenham club record for most goals in a season and 33 of those came in the league to secure him with the Golden Boot. He also won the PFA Player of the Year and Football Writers' Association Footballer of the Year awards that campaign. Allen joined from Queens Park Rangers in 1984. HE scored twice in his debut and went on to score 84 times in 135 games before being sold to Bordeaux in France in 1988. Allen played for the London Monarchs in NFL Europe in 1997 as a kicker and later had a stint as Tottenham caretaker manager.

10. At just 5-feet, 5-inches tall, English international winger Aaron Lennon was one of the smallest but speediest wingers to play in the Premier League. He began his career at hometown club Leeds United and became the youngest player in the Premier League at the time when making his debut in 2003. He joined Tottenham in 2005 and went on to score just over 30 goals in 367 appearances. He helped the team win the 2007-08 League Cup and was named the team's Player of the Year for 2008-09. Lennon joined Everton in 2015 and was playing for Süper Lig club Kayserispor in Turkey as of March 2021.

CHAPTER 8:

NOTABLE TRANSFERS/SIGNINGS

QUIZ TIME!

1. As of 2020, the club's highest ever transfer fee was spent on what player?

   a. Moussa Sissoko

   b. Giovani Lo Celso

   c. Davinson Sánchez

   d. Tanguy Ndombélé

2. Tottenham signed eight players from the German Bundesliga in 2018-19.

   a. True

   b. False

3. What was the club's most expensive signing in 2008-09, costing a reported £19.8 million?

   a. Luka Modrić

   b. David Bentley

   c. Roman Pavlyuchenko

   d. Robbie Keane

4. Which player did Tottenham sell for the club's highest transfer fee received as of 2020?

   a. Kyle Walker
   b. Dimitar Berbatov
   c. Gareth Bale
   d. Luka Modrić

5. What was the reported transfer fee the Spurs received for Kyle Walker?

   a. £41 million
   b. £55 million
   c. £38 million
   d. £47.43 million

6. Which club did Tanguy Ndombélé leave to join Tottenham?

   a. Toulouse FC
   b. Olympique Lyon
   c. Dijon FCO
   d. Atalanta

7. Michael Carrick was sold to Manchester United in 2006-07.

   a. True
   b. False

8. How much did Tottenham reportedly pay to purchase Davinson Sánchez?

   a. £29 million
   b. £32 million

c. £37.8 million

d. £45 million

9. To which club did the Spurs sell Christian Eriksen in 2019-20?

a. Liverpool FC

b. S.S.C. Napoli

c. Inter Milan

d. Atlético Madrid

10. How much was the transfer fee Tottenham reportedly received from Real Madrid for Luka Modrić?

a. £31.5 million

b. £27 million

c. £36 million

d. £22 million

11. Which club did the Spurs sign Moussa Sissoko from?

a. West Bromwich Albion

b. Paris FC

c. Newcastle United

d. EA Guingamp

12. Tottenham signed Son Heung-min for a reported fee of £7 million.

a. True

b. False

13. What was the reported transfer fee the Spurs paid to acquire Tanguy Ndombélé?

a. £30 million

b. £42 million

c. £47 million

d. £54 million

14. Who was the club's most expensive signing in 2012-13 for £17 million?

    a. Gylfi Sigurðsson

    b. Jan Vertonghen

    c. Hugo Lloris

    d. Mousa Dembélé

15. How much did the Spurs reportedly receive from Manchester United for Dimitar Berbatov?

    a. £23 million

    b. £28 million

    c. £34.2 million

    d. £40 million

16. Tottenham sold Gareth Bale to Real Madrid for a reported fee of £105 million.

    a. True

    b. False

17. From which side did Tottenham sign Darren Brent in 2007-08?

    a. Swansea City FC

    b. Charlton Athletic

    c. Middlesbrough FC

    d. Preston North End

18. Who was the club's most expensive signing in 2017-18?

    a. Davinson Sánchez

    b. Lucas Moura

    c. Serge Aurier

    d. Fernando Llorente

19. What was the reported transfer fee Tottenham paid to sign Giovani Lo Celso?

    a. £20 million

    b. £25 million

    c. £28.8 million

    d. £33 million

20. Gary Mabbutt was the Spurs' first £1 million purchase.

    a. True

    b. False

QUIZ ANSWERS

1. D – Tanguy Ndombélé

2. B – False

3. B – David Bentley

4. C – Gareth Bale

5. D – £47.43 million

6. B – Olympique Lyon

7. A – True

8. C – £37.8 million

9. C – Inter Milan

10. A – £31.5 million

11. C – Newcastle United

12. B – False

13. D – £54 million

14. D – Mousa Dembélé

15. C – £34.2 million

16. B – False

17. B – Charlton Athletic

18. A – Davinson Sánchez

19. C – £28.8 million

20. B – False

DID YOU KNOW?

1. As of March 2021, the five most expensive transfer fees paid by Tottenham are: Midfielder Tanguy Ndombélé from Olympique Lyon in 2019-20 for £54 million, defenders Davinson Sánchez from Ajax Amsterdam in 2017-18 for £37.8 million, midfielder Moussa Sissoko from Newcastle United in 2016-17 for £31.5 million, Midfielder Giovani Lo Celso from Real Betis in 2020-21 for £28.8 million, Winger Steven Bergwijn from PSV Eindhoven in 2019-20 for £27 million, forward Roberto Soldado from Valencia CF in 2013-14 for £27 million, defenders Sergio Reguilón from Real Madrid in 2020-21 for £27 million, forward Erik Lamela from AS Roma in 2013-14 for £27 million, forward Heung-min Son from Bayer 04 Leverkusen in 2015-16 for £27 million.

2. As of March 2021, the top five transfer fees received by the club are as follows: forward Gareth Bale to Real Madrid in 2013-14 for £90.9 million, defenders Kyle Walker to Manchester City in 2017-18 for £47.43 million, forward Dimitar Berbatov to Manchester United in 2008-09 for £34.2 million, midfielder Luka Modrić to Real Madrid in 2012-13 for £31.5 million, midfielder Michael Carrick to Manchester United in 2006-07 for £24.48 million.

3. English international defender and former Spurs' captain Sol Campbell joined arch-rivals Arsenal in 2001, just before his contract expired, and the club's fans weren't too happy about it. The Spurs had offered Campbell a new deal that would have seen him become the highest-paid player in club history. After publicly stating that he intended to remain at White Hart Lane, Campbell signed with Arsenal. And, to make matters worse, the Spurs didn't receive a penny since it was a free transfer. Some fans hung Campbell in effigy and constantly ridiculed him whenever the sides met because he had earlier claimed he'd never play for Arsenal.

4. Croatian international midfielder Luka Modrić enraged many Spurs' supporters by trying to force a move after signing a six-year deal in 2010. A year later, he learned that Chelsea was interested in him when the Spurs rejected three bids from their neighbors. Modrić claimed Tottenham agreed to sell him if a big club was interested. He refused to play in the Spurs' 2011-12 season opener but changed his mind when he realized he wouldn't be paid. He played the campaign but in 2012-13 he sat out the preseason to once again try to force a move. He was fined £80,000 and eventually sold to Real Madrid for £31.5 million, which was reportedly £10 million less than what Chelsea offered.

5. Winger David Bentley was expected to be an elite player after breaking in with Arsenal in 2002, as many fans compared him to David Beckham. He played just one

league match with Arsenal, though, while spending most of his time on loan. Blackburn signed him in 2006 and Bentley netted 13 goals in 88 league outings there. Tottenham then signed the young striker for a reported £15 million in July 2008, but he made just 42 league appearances and tallied 2 goals. He was then loaned to Birmingham City, West Ham United, FC Rostov of Russia, and Blackburn. Bentley retired in 2014 at the age of 29 with 30 career league goals in 267 club games and he played seven times for England.

6. In June 1988, Paul Stewart became the club's first million-pound signing when he arrived from Manchester City for a reported £1.5 million. At the time, Stewart also became the costliest player in the history of the Second Division. He began his career with the Spurs as a striker but then converted to the midfield. Stewart scored the team's first goal in the 1990-91 FA Cup final victory over Nottingham Forest and was then transferred to Liverpool in July 1992 for a reported £2.3million.

7. When Gareth Bale was sold to Real Madrid in 2013 for £90.9 million, the fee set a new world record at the time. The Welsh international had arrived in May 2007 from Southampton for a reported £5 million, which could rise to £10 million depending on incentives. Bale's first two seasons at the Spurs were plagued by injury but he proved to be one of the world's premier talents and notched 55 goals in just over 200 games. He was named Tottenham Young Player of the Year in 2009-10 and 2010-

11, as well as Player of the Year in 2012-13. Bale won numerous team and individual awards with Real Madrid before returning to the Spurs on a season-long loan in September 2020. Bale proceeded to net 10 goals in his first 22 appearances as of March 2021.

8. Cameroon international winger Clinton N'Jie signed from Lyon for a reported £8.3 million in 2015 but suffered a serious knee injury before Christmas. He returned in May 2016 and made a total of eight substitute appearances in the Premier League with one appearance in the League Cup and five in the Europa League without scoring. After those 14 games, he was loaned to Marseille in August 2016 and sold to the club a year later for an undisclosed fee.

9. Belgian international midfielder Jonathan Blondel joined from Excelsior Mouscron in August 2002 on a free transfer but was gone by January 2004 when he joined Club Brugge. In between, he made his Premier League debut in August 2002 at the age of 18 years and 150 days and didn't play again until coming on as a substitute in November 2003. Blondel's two appearances for Tottenham lasted approximately 37 minutes in total. However, the club made a £1.08 million profit when he was sold to Brugge.

10. Tottenham's current transfer record fee of £54 million was spent on French international midfielder Tanguy Ndombélé when he was bought from Lyon in July 2019. The fee may go up in the future depending on the add-on

clauses attached to the deal. He scored in his Premier League debut but played just 21 league games in his first season and 29 in all competitions. His play improved early in 2020-21 and he had scored 6 goals in his first 35 appearances as of March 2021.

CHAPTER 9:

ODDS & ENDS

QUIZ TIME!

1. The most games the Spurs have won in a domestic league season as of 2020 is?

   a. 26
   b. 29
   c. 31
   d. 35

2. Tottenham's rivalry with Arsenal was intensified after Arsenal was promoted to the First Division in 1919 instead of Tottenham.

   a. True
   b. False

3. The club's biggest domestic league win was a 9-0 victory against which side?

   a. Swansea City FC
   b. Portsmouth FC

c. West Ham United

d. Bristol Rovers

4. How many matches did the squad draw in the 1968-69 domestic league season?

a. 20

b. 17

c. 15

d. 11

5. Who was the youngest player to make an appearance with the first team, at 16 years and 163 days old?

a. Stephen Carr

b. John Bostock

c. Dane Scarlett

d. Alfie Devine

6. How many goals did the team score in the 1960-61 domestic league season?

a. 96

b. 111

c. 115

d. 124

7. The club first played its matches on public land, meaning they had to mark the pitch themselves.

a. True

b. False

8. Tottenham was hammered 8-0 by which club in the 1995 Intertoto Cup?

    a. Juventus
    b. Borussia Dortmund
    c. AC Milan
    d. FC Köln

9. The Spurs' biggest domestic league defeat was a 7-0 thrashing by what club?

    a. Manchester United
    b. Liverpool FC
    c. Chelsea FC
    d. Arsenal

10. The most losses by the Spurs in a domestic league season as of 2020 is?

    a. 26
    b. 22
    c. 18
    d. 15

11. The Spurs' biggest margin of victory was a 13-2 win against which club in the 1960-61 FA Cup?

    a. Crewe Alexandria
    b. Charlton Athletic
    c. Burnley FC
    d. Aston Villa

12. As of 2020, the Spurs have never scored 100 goals in a Premier League season.

a. True

b. False

13. What is the most goals Tottenham has scored in a domestic league game as of 2020?

    a. 7

    b. 8

    c. 10

    d. 12

14. Who was the oldest Spurs player to make an appearance at the age of 42 years and 176 days?

    a. Teddy Sheringham

    b. Danny Blanchflower

    c. Ray Clemence

    d. Brad Friedel

15. How many Spurs have played for the English men's national team as of January 2021?

    a. 66

    b. 73

    c. 78

    d. 83

16. Tottenham's rivalry with Arsenal is known as the "North London Derby."

    a. True

    b. False

17. The Spurs' biggest Premier League defeat as of 2020 was a 7-1 walloping by which side?

    a. Liverpool FC
    b. Newcastle United
    c. Chelsea FC
    d. Sheffield United

18. Tottenham set a club attendance record in the 2016-17 UEFA Champions League against which club?

    a. AS Monaco FC
    b. FC Barcelona
    c. Bayer Leverkusen
    d. Paris Saint-Germaine

19. Which year was Tottenham's women's soccer team founded?

    a. 1993
    b. 1990
    c. 1985
    d. 1980

20. The Spurs' final match at White Hart Lane was against Manchester City.

    a. True
    b. False

QUIZ ANSWERS

1. C – 31

2. A – True

3. D – Bristol Rovers

4. B – 17

5. D – Alfie Devine

6. C – 115

7. A – True

8. D – FC Köln

9. B – Liverpool FC

10. B - 22

11. A – Crewe Alexandria

12. A – True

13. C – 10

14. D – Brad Friedel

15. C – 78

16. A – True

17. B – Newcastle United

18. C – Bayer Leverkusen

19. C – 1985

20. B – False

DID YOU KNOW?

1. The club's early games were held at the Tottenham Marshes, which was public land. This meant the team had to prepare and mark out the pitch by themselves. However, fights would occasionally break out with other teams who wanted to use the land at the same time. The first time a Spurs game was covered by the local press was at this venue on October 6, 1883, when they thrashed the Brownlow Rovers 9-0.

2. The outfit's current home ground is Tottenham Hotspur Stadium in London, which has a seating capacity of 62,850 for soccer. The club moved from White Hart Lane into its new digs in 2019 and its first senior outing was against Crystal Palace on April 3.

3. The first competitive game at White Hart Lane in September 1899 was a 1-0 victory over Queens Park Rangers in the Southern League. The game receipts totaled just over £329, and a home season ticket was under £1. In May 2017, the Spurs played at White Hart Lane for the final time, and edged Manchester United 2-1. The team's home matches were then moved to Wembley Stadium while a new stadium was being built in Tottenham.

4. Shortly afterward, a new club attendance record of 85,512 was set in a clash against Bayer Leverkusen in a European Champions League contest at Wembley. The previous

crowd record was 75,038 against Sunderland in the sixth round of the FA Cup at White Hart Lane.

5. Tottenham's current training ground at Bulls Cross in Enfield was opened in 2012. The 77-acre venue contains 15 grass pitches and several artificial pitches. including one indoors. It has medical facilities, gyms, hydrotherapy and swimming pools, a dining area, and classrooms for schoolboy and academy players. There's also a 45-bedroom players lodge with catering and rehabilitation facilities.

6. The club's emblem is a cockerel standing upon a football with a Latin motto *Audere est Facere* ("To Dare Is to Do"). The club used the Spurs as a team symbol in 1900 and it evolved into a fighting cock after a former player named William James Scott created a bronze cast of a cockerel standing on a football. The cast was placed on top of the West Stand at White Hart Lane in 1910 and it soon became part of the club's identity.

7. In 1983, Tottenham became the first European soccer club to float shares on the London Stock Exchange. The club became a limited company in the late 1800s, as the Tottenham Hotspur Football and Athletic Company Ltd, and shares were sold to raise money. In November 1982, a Spurs fan named Irving Scholar bought 25 percent of the club for £600,000 and then floated it on the stock exchange.

8. After Irving Scholar took over the majority of shares in Tottenham Hotspur, the club endured financial difficulties. Former player Terry Venables and businessman Alan Sugar bought the club in 1991 with Sugar being the majority owner. He then sold the majority of his shares in the club in February 2001 to ENIC International Ltd, which is an investment company established by British billionaire Joe Lewis and his partner Daniel Levy. In January 2012, the stocks were de-listed, and the club became a private entity, with ENIC owning approximately 85 percent.

9. Tottenham also has a women's soccer team that was founded in 1985 as Broxbourne Ladies. The club began to use the Tottenham Hotspur name in 1991-92 when it competed in the fourth-tier London and South East Women's Regional Football League. The team won the league title in 2007-08, won the FA Women's Premier League Southern Division in 2016-17, and was promoted to the FA Women's Super League 2. Tottenham Hotspur Women were promoted to the top-flight FA Women's Super League in 2020, and currently play their home games at The Hive Stadium in Canons Park.

10. Spurs fans sing several songs to support the team, "Glory Glory Tottenham Hotspur" is one of the most popular. It originated in 1961 after the club won the FA Cup and league double and entered the European Cup. It is sung to the tune of the hymn "Glory Glory Hallelujah."

CHAPTER 10:

DOMESTIC COMPETITION

QUIZ TIME!

1. How many times has Tottenham won the First Division/ Premier League as of 2020?

   a. 1
   b. 2
   c. 4
   d. 5

2. Tottenham was the first British club to win a domestic FA Cup and First Division double since 1897.

   a. True
   b. False

3. Which year did Tottenham win their first FA Charity Shield?

   a. 1919
   b. 1921
   c. 1930
   d. 1951

4. The Spurs defeated which club to win their first FA Cup?

    a. Reading FC
    b. West Bromwich Albion
    c. Burnley FC
    d. Sheffield United

5. Tottenham shared the 1967 FA Charity Shield with which side?

    a. Manchester United
    b. Aston Villa
    c. Everton FC
    d. Liverpool FC

6. How many times has Tottenham won the League Cup as of 2020?

    a. 7
    b. 4
    c. 3
    d. 1

7. Tottenham won the second-tier Second Division title three times.

    a. True
    b. False

8. Which season did the club win its first domestic double?

    a. 1950-51
    b. 1958-59
    c. 1960-61
    d. 1964-65

9. Who did the Spurs bounce to win the 1970-71 League Cup?

    a. Nottingham Forest
    b. Leeds United
    c. Aston Villa
    d. Manchester City

10. How many times did the club win the Southern League title?

    a. 0
    b. 1
    c. 2
    d. 3

11. Which season did the club win its first Southern League crown?

    a. 1896-97
    b. 1898-99
    c. 1899-00
    d. 1903-04

12. The Spurs were two-time winners of the Sheriff of London Charity Shield.

    a. True
    b. False

13. How many times did the team win the London Challenge Cup?

    a. 5
    b. 7

c. 8

d. 11

14. Which club did the squad defeat for the 1962 FA Charity Shield?

    a. Ipswich Town

    b. Blackburn Rovers

    c. Wolverhampton Wanders

    d. Football Association XI

15. What player was named Man of the Match for the Spurs in the 2007-08 League Cup final?

    a. Aaron Lennon

    b. Dimitar Berbatov

    c. Robbie Keane

    d. Jonathan Woodgate

16. Tottenham won the Western League three times.

    a. True

    b. False

17. Which side did the club defeat in the 1960-61 FA Cup final?

    a. Manchester City

    b. Leicester City FC

    c. Burnley FC

    d. Blackburn Rovers

18. How many times have the Spurs shared the FA Charity/ Community Shield as of 2020?

a. 0

b. 1

c. 3

d. 6

19. Which club did Tottenham defeat in the 2007-08 League Cup final?

    a. Sunderland AFC

    b. Liverpool FC

    c. Leicester City FC

    d. Chelsea FC

20. The Spurs have won the FA Cup eight times as of 2020.

    a. True

    b. False

QUIZ ANSWERS

1. B – 2

2. A – True

3. B – 1921

4. D – Sheffield United

5. A – Manchester United

6. B – 4

7. B – False

8. C – 1960-61

9. C – Aston Villa

10. B – 1

11. C – 1899-00

12. A – True

13. C – 8

14. A – Ipswich Town

15. D – Jonathan Woodgate

16. B – False

17. B – Leicester City FC

18. C – 3

19. D – Chelsea FC

20. A – True

DID YOU KNOW?

1. Tottenham has won two top-flight league titles and two second-tier league championships. The squad has captured eight FA Cup trophies, four English League Cups, and seven FA Charity/Community Shields. Their highest finish in the Premier League came in 2016-17 when they earned a club-record 86 points with 26 wins, 8 draws, and just 4 losses. They were relegated from the top-flight to the second-tier four times, 1914-15, 1927-38, 1934-45, and 1976-77.

2. The club won the top-flight First Division title in 1950-51 and 1960-61, and topped the second-tier Second Division in 1919-20, and 1949-50. The FA Cup triumphs came in 1900-01, 1920-21, 1960-61, 1961-62, 1966-67, 1980-81, 1981-82, and 1990-91. The squad won the League Cup in 1970-71, 1972-73, 1998-99, and 2007-08. They captured the FA Charity/Community Shield in 1921, 1951, 1961, 1962, 1967, 1981, and 1991, and shared the honor in 1961, 1981, and 1991 because the games ended in a draw.

3. Tottenham has also won several minor pieces of domestic silverware including, Southern League Champions in 1899-1900, Western League Champions in1903-1904, London League Premier Division Champions in 1902-1903, Football League South C Division Champions in 1939-1940, Football League South Champions in 1943-

1944 and 1944-1945, Southern District Charity Cup Winners in 1901-1902, 1904-1905 (shared), and 1906-1907, Dewar Shield Winners in 1901-1902 and 1933-1934, and London Challenge Cup Winners in 1910-1911 and 1928-1929.

4. The main rivalries for Tottenham are the other London-based clubs, with the rivalry against Arsenal, known as the North London Derby, arguably being the most heated. The rivalry began back in 1913 when Arsenal moved to Arsenal Stadium in Highbury, and it intensified in 1919 when the club was promoted to the First Division by a vote instead of Tottenham. The Spurs' other London rivals include Chelsea, West Ham United, Fulham, and Crystal Palace.

5. Tottenham currently owns or shares several national domestic soccer records, including most consecutive wins from the start of a top-flight season, with 11 in 1960-61, most wins in a league campaign, with 31 in 42 games in 1960-61, most Premier League goals scored by a player in a calendar year, with 39 by Harry Kane in 2017, most points in a Second Division season (2 points for a win), with 70 in 1919–20, first team to concede 1,000 goals in the Premier League, and most goals scored in a Premier League game, with 9.

6. The club's record domestic wins are highest-scoring win, record cup victory, and biggest home win, 13-2 vs Crewe Alexandra in the FA Cup in 1960, biggest league victory,

9-0 vs Bristol Rovers in the Second Division in 1977, biggest Premier League win, 9-1 vs Wigan Athletic in 2009, and most league goals scored in a 10-4 win vs Everton in October 1958. Their record domestic away wins were 7-0 vs Tranmere Rovers in the FA Cup in 2019, 6-0 vs Oldham Athletic in the League Cup in 2004, and 7-1 vs Hull City in the Premier League in 2017.

7. The Spurs' biggest defeats in domestic competition are most league goals conceded, 8-2 vs Derby County in the First Division in1976, record league defeat, 7-0 vs Liverpool in the First Division in 1978, 7-1 vs Newcastle United in 1996, 6-0 vs Sheffield United in March 1993, and 6-0 vs Manchester City in 2013, record cup loss, 6-1 vs Newcastle United in the FA Cup in 1999, and record home defeat, 6-0 vs Sunderland in the First Division in 1914 and 6-0 vs Arsenal in the First Division in 1935.

8. Other current club records and milestones include 854 appearances and 655 league appearances by Steve Perryman, most league points (2 points for a win), 70 in the Second Division in 1919-20, most league points (3 points for a win), 86 in the Premier League in 2016-17, most league goals, 115 in the First Division in 1960-61, youngest scorer and youngest first-team player, Alfie Devine at 16 years, 163 days in January 2021, and oldest first-team player, goalkeeper Brad Friedel at 42 years, 176 days in November 2013.

9. The players with the most career appearances for Tottenham are Steve Perryman, 854, Gary Mabbutt, 611, goalkeeper Pat Jennings, 590, Tom Morris, 523, Cyril Knowles, 506, Glenn Hoddle, 490, Ted Ditchburn, 452, Alan Gilzean, 439, Jimmy Dimmock, 438, and Phil Beal, 420.

10. As of March 2021, players who have earned the most international caps for England while playing with the Spurs are 51, Harry Kane, 49, Jermain Defoe, 44, Eric Dier, 44, Glenn Hoddle, 42, Jimmy Greaves, 40, Sol Campbell, 38, Gary Lineker, 38, Teddy Sheringham, 37, Dele Alli, 37, Paul Robinson, 36, Chris Waddle, 35, Alan Mullery, 34, Martin Peters, 31, Alf Ramsey, 30, Darren Anderton, 29, Danny Rose, 27, Kyle Walker, 24, Martin Chivers, 23, Maurice Norman, 21, Ledley King, 21, Aaron Lennon, 21, Vivian Woodward, and 20, Paul Gascoigne.

CHAPTER 11:

EUROPE AND BEYOND

QUIZ TIME!

1. How many major international trophies have the Spurs won as of 2020?

   a. 9

   b. 6

   c. 4

   d. 2

2. The 1962-63 UEFA Cup Winners' Cup was the first international tournament Tottenham participated in.

   a. True

   b. False

3. What was the first team the Spurs met in a major European competition?

   a. Feyenoord

   b. KS Górnik Zabrze

   c. Dukla Prague

   d. S.L. Benfica

4. Who is the club's leading goal scorer in European competitions as of March 2021?

   a. Harry Kane
   b. Son Heung-min
   c. Jermaine Defoe
   d. Martin Chivers

5. Which club did the Spurs defeat in the 1962-63 UEFA Cup Winners' Cup final?

   a. SK Slovan Bratislava
   b. Olympique Lyon
   c. OFK Beograd
   d. Atlético Madrid

6. Which season did Tottenham hoist the Anglo-Italian League Cup?

   a. 1978-79
   b. 1975-76
   c. 1971-72
   d. 1969-70

7. Tottenham had won 253 games in all UEFA competitions as of March 11, 2021.

   a. True
   b. False

8. How many goals did Jermaine Defoe score for the club in European competitions?

   a. 30
   b. 26

c. 23

d. 19

9. The Spurs became the first team to score 2 or more goals in every European Champions League group match in which season?

   a. 2008-09

   b. 2010-11

   c. 2014-15

   d. 2018-19

10. Tottenham faced which club in the 2019 UEFA Champions League final?

    a. Juventus

    b. Liverpool FC

    c. Ajax

    d. FC Barcelona

11. How many goals had Harry Kane scored in European competitions as of March 15, 2021?

    a. 22

    b. 27

    c. 30

    d. 38

12. Tottenham was the first British club to win a UEFA tournament.

    a. True

    b. False

13. Which club did the Spurs NOT face on their way to the 1971-72 UEFA Cup final?

    a. FC Porto
    b. AC Milan
    c. FC Nantes
    d. UTA Arad

14. How many goals did Martin Chivers score in European matches?

    a. 27
    b. 25
    c. 22
    d. 19

15. Which side did the Spurs face in the 1984 UEFA Cup final?

    a. HNK Hajduk Split
    b. RSC Anderlecht
    c. Spartak Moscow
    d. Bayern Munich

16. Tottenham has won the UEFA Cup twice as of 2020.

    a. True
    b. False

17. The Spurs beat which club to win their only Anglo-Italian League Cup?

    a. AS Roma
    b. Torino FC

   c. S.S.C. Napoli

   d. Bologna FC

18. Who scored the winning goal in the 1962-63 UEFA Cup Winners' Cup final?

   a. Jimmy Greaves

   b. John White

   c. Terry Dyson

   d. Bobby Smith

19. Tottenham downed what side to win its first UEFA Cup?

   a. Red Star Belgrade

   b. Real Madrid

   c. Paris Saint-Germain

   d. Wolverhampton Wanderers

20. Tottenham's opponent in the 1984 UEFA Cup final, RSC Anderlecht, was later found to have bribed their way to victory in the semi-finals.

   a. True

   b. False

QUIZ ANSWERS

1. C – 4

2. B – False

3. B – KS Górnik Zabrze

4. A – Harry Kane

5. D – Atlético Madrid

6. C – 1971-72

7. B – False

8. C – 23

9. B – 2010-11

10. B – Liverpool FC

11. D – 38

12. A – True

13. A – FC Porto

14. C – 22

15. B – RSC Anderlecht

16. A – True

17. B – Torino FC

18. B – John White

19. D – Wolverhampton Wanderers

20. A – True

DID YOU KNOW?

1. When it comes to European competition, Tottenham was crowned the European Cup Winners' Cup champions in 1962-1963 and captured the UEFA Cup in 1971-1972 and 1983-1984. The club also won the minor Anglo-Italian League Cup-Winners' Cup in 1971-72.

2. Tottenham was the first British club to win a UEFA competition when they hoisted the European Cup Winners' Cup in 1963, and then became the first in Britain to win the UEFA Cup/ Europa League in 1972. This made it the first British club to win two different European Trophies. The club holds the British record of eight consecutive victories in major European competition as well as the most games played in the UEFA Cup/ Europa League by a British side. They were also the first team to score 2 or more goals in every European Champions League group match in the 2010-11 campaign.

3. As of March 15, 2021, the team's top scorers in European competition were Harry Kane, 38, Jermain Defoe, 23, Martin Chivers, 22, Son Heung, min, 20, Mark Falco, 13, Alan Gilzean, 13, Martin Peters, 13, Dimitar Berbatov, 12, Erik Lamela, 12, Gareth Bale, 11, and Christian Eriksen, 10. It should be noted that Kane, Min, Lamela, and Bale are still playing with the club.

4. The Spurs won the 1962-63 European Cup Winners' Cup by downing the defending champions, Atlético Madrid of Spain, 5-1 in the final at Feijenoord Stadion in Rotterdam, Holland. Jimmy Greaves and Terry Dyson both scored twice for the team in front of 49,000 fans and John White tallied once. Bill Brown was the goalkeeper on the day.

5. The 1971-72 Europa League final was a two-legged affair between Tottenham and fellow English side Wolverhampton Wanderers. It was the inaugural final of the competition, with the Spurs winning 3-2 on aggregate. They won the first leg 2-1 away with Martin Chivers scoring both goals including the winner with just three minutes remaining and Pat Jennings playing in goal. They drew the second leg 1-1 at home with Allan Mullery scoring the goal and Jennings playing in goal again.

6. The 1983-84 UEFA Cup final was also a two-legged contest, between Tottenham and Anderlecht of Belgium, the defending champions. The score was tied 2-2 on aggregate and had to be decided by a penalty shootout. The teams drew 1-1 in the first leg in Belgium, with Paul Miller scoring for the Spurs and Anderlecht's Morten Olsen equalizing in the 85th minute. The second leg was also a 1-1 draw with Graham Roberts tying the match in the 84th minute. The Spurs won the shootout 4-3 with Tony Parks playing in goal for both games.

7. Anderlecht's journey to the 1983-84 UEFA Cup final was controversial, as it was reported in 1997 the club's chairman had paid a £27,000 bribe to the referee to guarantee the outcome of their 3-2 aggregate semi-final win over Nottingham Forest. Anderlecht was awarded a dubious penalty while a last-minute Forest goal was disallowed. In 2016, it emerged that UEFA had known about the bribe since 1993 but no action was taken until the information became public. Anderlecht was then suspended from the 1998-99 UEFA Cup, but the ban was overturned by the Court of Arbitration for Sport, it said UEFA's Executive Committee didn't have the authority to ban the club.

8. The first leg of the Spurs' semi-final away to Hajduk Split of Croatia was also controversial. A Hajduk supporter named Ante Baraba ran onto the pitch before the kickoff and snapped the neck of a live rooster, which is the famous club cockerel symbol of Tottenham. Hajduk won the game 2-1 but was fined for the incident and ordered to play their next home European game at least 300 kilometers away from its home ground.

9. The Anglo-Italian League Cup, also known as the Anglo-Italian League Cup Winners' Cup, was played between 1969 and 1976 between Italian and English teams. To qualify, an English team had to win the League Cup or FA Cup, while the Italian entrant was the Coppa Italia winner. This was a two-legged final which the Spurs won

3-0 in aggregate over Torino in 1971 after winning the first leg 1-0 in Italy and the second leg 2-0 at home.

10. Tottenham reached the 2018-19 European Champions League final in Madrid, Spain, where they took on fellow Premier League side Liverpool FC. It was the Spurs' first European Cup/ Champions League final, but it didn't end well, as they were downed 2-0. Liverpool's Mohamed Salah scored on a penalty kick after just 106 seconds and Divock Origi added some insurance with three minutes remaining.

CHAPTER 12:

TOP SCORERS

QUIZ TIME!

1. Who was the club's all-time leading goal scorer in all competitions as of March 2021?

    a. Bobby Smith

    b. Harry Kane

    c. Martin Chivers

    d. Jimmy Greaves

2. Tottenham has had 10 different players lead the First Division/Premier League in scoring as of 2020.

    a. True

    b. False

3. Who was the first player to lead the team in scoring, back in 1896-97?

    a. Tom Pratt

    b. John Cameron

    c. Bob Clements

    d. Bill Joyce

4. How many goals did George Hunt tally in 198 matches in all competitions for the Spurs?

   a. 105
   b. 119
   c. 138
   d. 152

5. Who led the squad with 21 goals in the 2012-13 domestic league?

   a. Gareth Bale
   b. Emmanuel Adebayor
   c. Harry Kane
   d. Jermaine Defoe

6. How many goals did Steve Archibald score to be the joint Golden Boot winner in 1980-81?

   a. 24
   b. 20
   c. 18
   d. 15

7. As of March 2021, Jimmy Greaves was the all-time leading scorer in the top flight of English football.

   a. True
   b. False

8. Which player led the Spurs and the Premier League in goals in 1992-93?

   a. Jürgen Klinsmann
   b. Paul Gascoigne

c. Gary Lineker

d. Teddy Sheringham

9. How many times did Jimmy Greaves win a Golden Boot with Tottenham?

a. 1

b. 3

c. 4

d. 6

10. Who holds the club record for most goals scored in a season in all competitions as of 2020?

a. Jimmy Greaves

b. Clive Allen

c. Harry Kane

d. George Hunt

11. How many goals did Bobby Smith score in 317 matches in all competitions with the Spurs?

a. 240

b. 177

c. 223

d. 208

12. Bobby Smith was the first Tottenham player to lead the First Division in scoring with 36 goals.

a. True

b. False

13. Which two players led the club with 15 goals each in the 2007-08 Premier League?

    a. Robbie Keane and Dimitar Berbatov

    b. Darren Brent and Jermaine Jenas

    c. Gareth Bale and Steed Malbranque

    d. Jamie O'Hara and Tom Huddlestone

14. How many domestic league goals did Harry Kane score to lead the team in 2017-18?

    a. 41

    b. 36

    c. 30

    d. 28

15. Who led Tottenham in scoring for four seasons between 1970-71 and 1973-74?

    a. John Pratt

    b. Martin Chivers

    c. Martin Peters

    d. Alan Mullery

16. Harry Kane has won the Premier League Golden Boot four times with the club as of 2020.

    a. True

    b. False

17. How many goals did Jimmy Greaves score in all competitions with Tottenham?

    a. 229

    b. 235

c. 244

d. 266

18. Who led the side with 22 goals in the 1984-85 domestic league?

    a. Mark Falco

    b. Steve Archibald

    c. Clive Allen

    d. Garth Crooks

19. How many goals did Clive Allen notch in all competitions in 1986-87?

    a. 43

    b. 46

    c. 49

    d. 52

20. Harry Kane has led the squad in scoring every season since 2013-14.

    a. True

    b. False

QUIZ ANSWERS

1. D – Jimmy Greaves

2. B – False

3. C – Bob Clements

4. C – 138

5. A – Gareth Bale

6. B – 20

7. A – True

8. D – Teddy Sheringham

9. C – 4

10. B – Clive Allen

11. D – 208

12. A – True

13. A – Robbie Keane and Dimitar Berbatov

14. C – 30

15. B – Martin Chivers

16. B – False

17. D – 266

18. A – Mark Falco

19. C – 49

20. B – False

DID YOU KNOW?

1. Teddy Sheringham was one of the club's greatest finishers, with 124 goals in 277 appearances, 97 of the goals came in the league. He first joined the club in 1992 from Nottingham Forest, and played till 1997 before joining Manchester United, and he returned from 2001 to 2003 before joining Portsmouth. The English international won the inaugural Premier League Golden Boot in 1992-93, with 22 goals in 41 games, 21 of them coming with the Spurs and 1 with Forest. Sheringham was the Spurs' Player of the Year for 1994-95 and was inducted into the English Football Hall of Fame in 2009.

2. Alan Gilzean joined the side in December 1964 for a reported £72,500 from Dundee United after turning down offers from Sunderland and Torino. He scored 133 goals for the team in 439 games and formed an excellent partnership with Jimmy Greaves. The Scottish international stayed for a decade before joining Aldershot in 1974. Gilzean was known as "The King of White Hart Lane" and helped the squad win two League Cups an FA Cup, an FA Charity Shield, and the UEFA Cup.

3. After briefly playing with Colchester United, forward Len Duquemin joined the Spurs and notched 134 goals in 307 outings until 1957 when he joined Bedford Town. Known as "Reliable Len" because of his consistent play and hard

work, he helped the team win the Second Division title in 1949-40 and the First Division crown the very next season. He retired in 1962 and later ran a pub in Hertfordshire.

4. With 138 goals in 198 contests for Tottenham, England international George Hunt remains one of the side's top-10 scorers. He arrived from Chesterfield in June 1930 and spent seven seasons with the club before joining Arsenal in 1937, becoming the first player to move from the team to Arsenal since Peter Kyle in 1906. He led the Spurs in scoring for three consecutive seasons, from 1931-32 to 1933-34, and his 32 league goals in 1932-33 helped the side earn promotion to the First Division. Hunt later became a coach with Bolton Wanderers and helped the side win the FA Cup in 1957-58.

5. Although he was just 5-feet, 7-inches tall, English international striker Jermain Defoe tallied 143 times in 363 outings with the club. He joined in February 2004 from West Ham United and was the team's Player of the Year for 2004. Defoe joined Portsmouth in January 2008 for a season and returned to Tottenham in January 2009. He joined Toronto FC in Canada in January 2014 but remained with the Spurs on loan until the end of February. Defoe helped Tottenham win the League Cup in 2007-08.

6. Cliff Jones was a Welsh international winger who netted 159 goals in 378 appearances and, like Jermain Defoe, was listed as being just 5-feet, 7-inches tall. He was a key member of Tottenham's 1960-61 FA Cup and First Division

Double-winning team, and he also won the 1961-62 FA Cup and 1962-63 European Cup Winners' Cup with the side as well as the 1966-67 FA Cup. Jones is considered one of the game's best wingers ever. He joined from Swansea Town in February 1958 and, in 1962, Juventus reportedly offered a world-record £125,000 to sign him. It was turned down, though, and Jones remained at White Hart Lane until joining Fulham in 1968.

7. After joining the Spurs in 1968 from Southampton, English international Martin Chivers proceeded to play 367 matches and netted 174 goals before joining Servette FC in Switzerland in 1976. He was the Spurs' top scorer in European competition for 39 years with 22 goals until Jermain Defoe passed him in November 2013 (Defoe was later passed by Harry Kane). Chivers won two League Cups and a UEFA Cup before leaving and later became a BBC radio announcer.

8. Center-forward Bobby Smith notched 13 goals in 15 games for England and contributed 208 for Tottenham in 317 contests, with 12 hat tricks. After five years with Chelsea, he arrived in December 1955 and remained until joining Brighton and Hove Albion in1964. He was part of the FA Cup and First Division double winners in 1960-1961, and also won the FA Cup in 1961-62 and the UEFA Cup Winners' Cup in 1962-1963. Smith scored in the final of both FA Cup victories and led the team in 1960-61 with 33 goals in 43 games.

9. As long as English international striker Harry Kane remains with Tottenham for the foreseeable future, he'll inevitably become the club's all-time leading scorer someday. He has led the side in scoring for the last six seasons, from 2014-15 through 2019-20, and won the Premier League Golden Boot in 2015-16 and 2016-17. Kane had 16 league goals after 26 games in 2020-21 and 26 in 37 total matches. As of March 2021, he had tallied 214 goals for the team in 324 games with a club-high 38 in Europe. He spent his youth career with the Spurs but was loaned out between 2010 and 2013 until becoming a regular in 2014-15.

10. English international striker Jimmy Greaves was still hanging onto his place as Tottenham's all-time leading scorer as of March 2021 with 266 goals in 379 matches. The prolific goal scorer joined from AC Milan in December 1961 and remained until joining West Ham United in 1970. He's the highest goal scorer in the history of English top-flight football with 357 goals and won six top-flight Golden Boot Awards. The member of the English Football Hall of Fame won two FA Cups and FA Charity Shields with the Spurs as well as the European Cup Winners' Cup. Greaves led or shared the team's scoring parade for eight straight seasons.

CONCLUSION

You've just had the history of Tottenham Hotspur FC presented to you from day one in 1882, right up to March 2021, when the club was battling for another fourth-place Premier League finish, and more European and domestic silverware.

It certainly has been a long and eventful journey, but it's nowhere near finished yet. We've provided the facts to you in an entertaining way, while hoping it's been an educational venture as well.

We've included numerous figures on the club's records, milestones, transfers, cup wins, and disappointments along the way, concerning its domestic and European performances.

With well over a century's worth of history, it's impossible to include every Spurs player and manager, and we hope we haven't missed too many of your favorites.

We've filled out pages with 12 different chapters based on the club's history, and each chapter offers a challenging trivia quiz. In addition, all of the chapters come with an amazing assortment of "Did You Know" facts.

By challenging yourself with the quizzes and absorbing all of the facts, you should now be as ready as ever to accept every Tottenham Hotspur trivia challenge that comes your way.

We also hope you'll be excited enough to share the book and information with fellow Spurs' supporters as a way to celebrate the club's glorious history.

With Tottenham continuing to entertain and thrill the fans season after season, the team couldn't have done it without your support.

Thank you for being one of the millions of loyal and passionate Spurs fans across the globe, and for taking the time to celebrate their club's history by reading our latest trivia and fact book.

Printed in Great Britain
by Amazon